ANCIENT CIVILIZATIONS

Ancient Maya

by Anita Ganeri

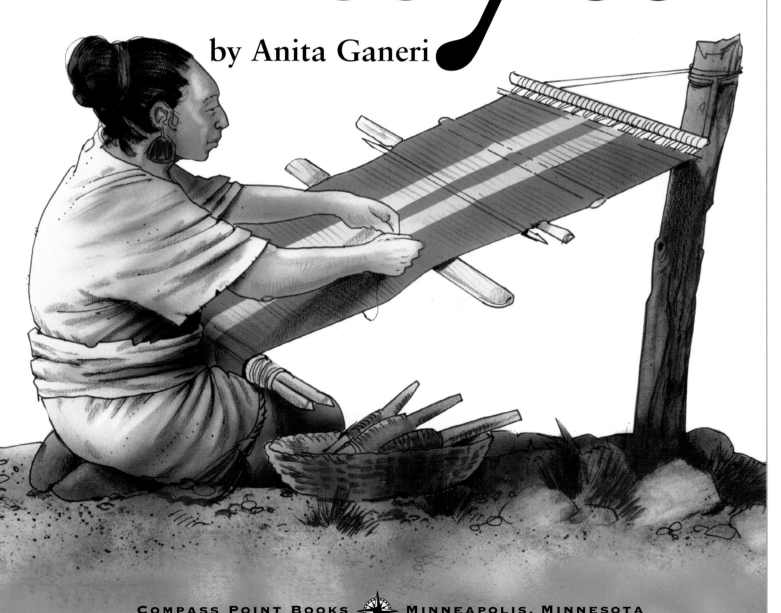

COMPASS POINT BOOKS ✦ MINNEAPOLIS, MINNESOTA

First American edition published in 2006 by
Compass Point Books
3109 West 50th St., #115
Minneapolis, MN 55410

ANCIENT MAYA
was produced by
David West Children's Books
7 Princeton Court
55 Felsham Road
London SW15 1AZ

Illustrator: Chris Forsey
Designer: Rob Shone
Editors: Kate Newport, Nick Healy
Page Production: Bobbie Nuytten
Content Adviser: Robert J. Sharer,
  Shoemaker Professor in Anthropology,
  University of Pennsylvania Museum

Visit Compass Point Books on the Internet at
www.compasspointbooks.com
or e-mail your request to
custserv@compasspointbooks.com

Library of Congress Cataloging-in-Publication Data
Ganeri, Anita, 1961-
   Ancient Maya / by Anita Ganeri.
      p. cm.—(Ancient civilizations)
   Includes bibliographical references and index.
   ISBN 0-7565-1677-3 (hardcover)
   1. Mayas—History—Juvenile literature. 2. Mayas—Material culture
—Juvenile literature. 3. Mayas—Social life and customs—Juvenile
literature.   I. Title. II. Series: Ancient civilizations (Minneapolis,
Minn.)
F1435.G168 2006
972'.01—dc22   2005025056

ISBN 0-7565-1758-3 (paperback)

√9/16/08

Contents

The Maya

The Maya civilization of Central America reached its peak about 1,700 years ago. It continued until about 500 years ago.

The Maya built great pyramids and worshipped many gods and goddesses. Their lords lived in great holy cities, and each city was ruled by its own king. The Maya also studied the stars and were the first people in Central America to write books. Although the Maya lived many years ago, we know a lot about their lives.

Look for this man digging up interesting items from the past, like this carving.

Who Were the Maya?

The ancient Maya people lived in Central America and southern Mexico for about 3,000 years.

The Maya all prayed to the same gods and spoke the same language. But they did not have one ruler or one capital city like most countries do today.

Each city had its own king, called the K'uhul Ajaw. He had total power over the city.

The kings lived in palaces. They made laws, kept up to date with news, and took gifts from local lords. When a king died, his eldest son replaced him.

The cities spent a lot of time at war with each other. Battles opened with the deafening sound of war drums, whistles, shell trumpets, and war cries.

Priests went with the armies and carried images of the Maya gods. This was thought to bring them good luck.

Jaguars were special animals in Maya times and their skins were valued. Jaguar skins were used to make costumes for Maya kings.

 *The Maya got a lot of ideas from the earlier Olmec people, who lived to the west. Like the Olmec, the Maya began to make stone carvings and build pyramid-shaped temples.*

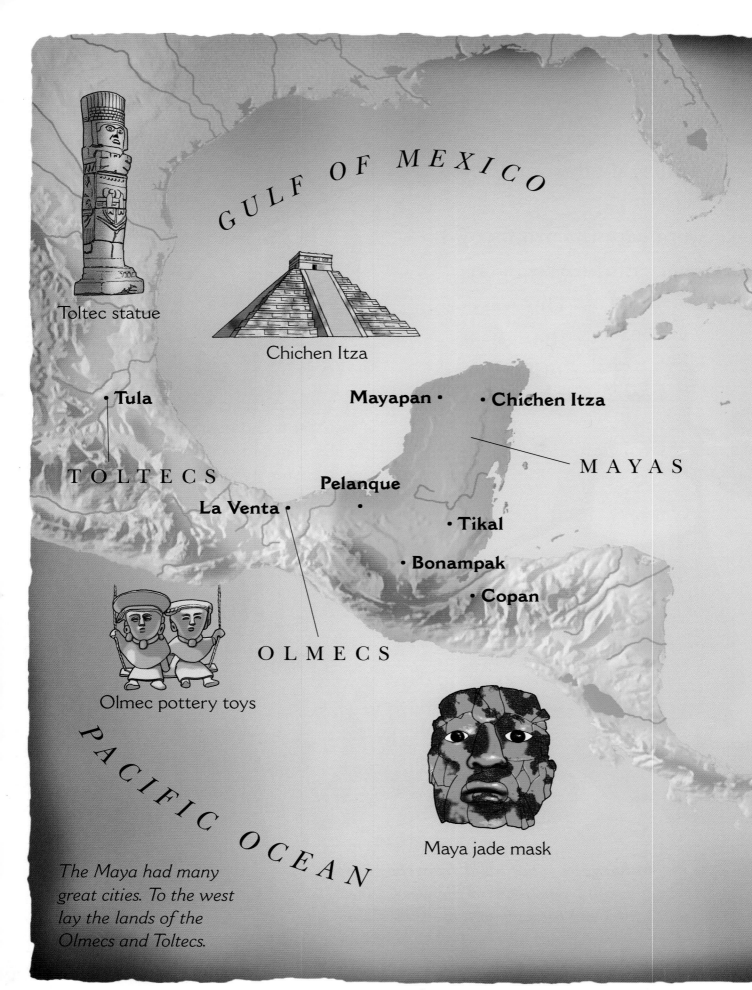

GULF OF MEXICO

Toltec statue

Chichen Itza

• Tula

Mayapan •   • **Chichen Itza**

T O L T E C S

M A Y A S

Pelanque
•

La Venta •

• **Tikal**

O L M E C S

• **Bonampak**

• **Copan**

Olmec pottery toys

Maya jade mask

PACIFIC OCEAN

The Maya had many great cities. To the west lay the lands of the Olmecs and Toltecs.

The Maya World

CARIBBEAN SEA

The Maya ruled parts of what is now Mexico, Belize, Guatemala, El Salvador, and Honduras.

Many of the biggest Maya cities were built in hot and humid rain forests. The Maya also lived in the hills.

The most famous period in Maya history was the Classic Period, about 2,000 years ago. The Maya built their most important cities, produced their best art, and made the most progress in their learning. They studied art, science, and mathematics.

Toward the end of the Classic Period, things began to change. Rival cities started to fight each other for land, trade routes, food, and jade.

Today we can learn a lot about the Maya from their buildings and stone carvings. A carving shows a group of Maya kings. We have also found Maya pottery, clay figures, and books.

Cities and Temples

The Maya lived in and around great cities such as Tikal, Chichen Itza, and Copan. They were built mainly for holy purposes and as gathering places for trade and entertainment. City dwellers were officials, priests, traders, and craftspeople. Many ordinary people lived on small farms and in villages just outside the cities.

Roads linked one city to another. Maya cities had large palaces built from polished or painted stone.

Maya cities also had narrow ball courts and very tall pyramid-shaped temples. These buildings were placed around huge squares, where holy ceremonies and prayer took place.

A Maya statue shows that the ballplayers wore lots of padding. This protected them against the solid, rubber ball. They had to hit the ball through a stone ring with their elbows, knees, hips, or forearms.

The sacred ball game of the Maya was played on a long, thin court that stood for Earth. The ball may have stood for the moon and sun.

Maya temples stood on top of giant pyramids with sloping terraces and a steep staircase. Sometimes a new temple was built around an old one. Some pyramids were more than 200 feet (61 meters) tall.

Maya Gods

The gods played a big part in the life of the Maya. People prayed to more than 160 gods and goddesses. Each of these ruled some part of daily life.

The chief god was Itzamna, or Lizard House, who was shown as an old man with a long nose. The Maya believed he had invented writing and he was god of learning and science.

His wife was called Ix Chel, or Lady Rainbow. She was goddess of weaving, the moon, medicine, and childbirth.

To keep the gods happy and to ask for their help, the Maya prayed and offered sacrifices such as jewelry and animals. Occasionally, humans were also sacrificed.

Maya priests held holy ceremonies, made sacrifices, and told the future. They also helped the kings with important city matters.

Many Maya gods were linked to nature and farming. A clay figure shows Chac, the god of rain. There was also a god of maize, the Maya's most important food, and a god of the sun.

Sometimes humans, including slaves and enemies, were sacrificed to the gods. The victims were thrown into a deep well.

Stories of the Hero Twins

The Maya told many stories about their gods.

One story said long ago there lived four brothers who were grandsons of the gods. The youngest sons, Hunahpu and Xbalanque, were very brave and clever, and were called the Hero Twins.

Their elder brothers were jealous of the twins and treated them like slaves. One day, the twins decided to teach them a lesson.

They tricked their brothers into climbing a tree to fetch some birds they had shot. Then the twins changed their brothers into monkeys and left them among the branches of the forest trees forever.

Another tale said the Hero Twins liked to play the sacred ball game all day long. This angered the Lords of the Underworld, who objected to all the loud noise above their heads. They made the twins go to the Underworld and play a game.

The Lords wanted to win so much that they cut off Hunahpu's head and stuck it above the ball court. They thought that Xbalanque could not play the game alone, but they were wrong.

Hunahpu quickly replaced his head with a turtle's head, and the twins won the game.

The Lords told the twins that they were sorry for trying to trick them. The Hero Twins were reborn in heaven as the sun and the moon.

Writing and Books

The Maya were the first people in Central America to start writing.

Words were not written with letters, but using a type of picture called hieroglyphs. Each symbol stood for a sound, an idea, or a whole word.

Maya writing was read from top to bottom and then from left to right. Priests and lords were the only people who could read.

The Maya also wrote books, and some of these still survive today. The books were written on paper made from fig tree bark, with covers made from jaguar skin.

Hieroglyphs were carved onto large stones called stelae. They were placed in front of important buildings. The stelae showed the main dates and events during a king's rule.

Each book was written on one long piece of bark and then folded to make pages. The books tell us about the Maya gods and goddesses, holy ceremonies, the stars, and lucky dates.

Many Maya books were written, but we only have four today. They were written in red and black ink using turkey feather quills.

The royal librarian, or "he of the holy books," was a very important person in a Maya city. He wore a long robe, and had long hair with a lot of quill pens tied to his forehead.

Counting and Calendars

The Maya also had a way of counting based on the number 20. They were skilled at mathematics and may have been the first people to have used a sign for zero.

Maya priests studied mathematics and astronomy, and invented two types of calendars. One was a sacred calendar of 260 days, used to determine lucky and unlucky days. The other was a calendar of 365 days, like the one we still use today. It was based on how long it took Earth to go around the sun.

Calendar stones showed important dates and events. This one shows how Earth began.

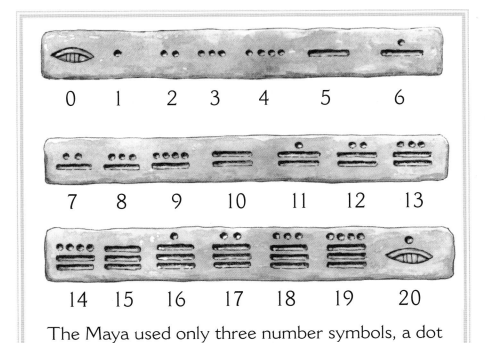

The Maya used only three number symbols, a dot for 1, a bar for 5, and a shell for zero. All other numbers were made up of these.

Maya priests were great astronomers. They studied how the stars and planets moved in the sky.

Farming and Food

Maya families worked their own land close to their houses. They were very good farmers.

In wet areas, they built canals to carry water to their fields. On hills, they built steps to stop the soil from falling down the slopes.

Maize, or corn, was the most important food in Maya times. Farmers also grew beans, squash, avocados, chili peppers, and fruits.

Maize was made into porridge, dumplings, and pancakes called tortillas. These were eaten with spicy turkey meat or bean stews and vegetables.

They raised turkeys for their meat and kept bees for their honey. They also hunted rabbits, piglike peccaries, and deer. They caught fish using nets, hooks, or bows and arrows.

Farmers cleared land by burning the trees and bushes. The ashes made the soil better for growing food.

Rich people drank hot chocolate. It was made from cocoa beans and served in pots. The poor could afford to drink only water.

Traders and Artists

Maya merchants were part of a trading system that extended across Central America.

They traded goods such as cotton, seashells, and sacred jaguar skins for jade and the bright feathers of the quetzal, a rain-forest bird.

Traveling over land took a very long time and was hard. Merchants had their own god to look after them.

On land, merchants carried goods mostly on their backs because they had no pack animals or wheeled carts or wagons. On the sea and on rivers, they traveled by dugout canoe.

Merchants used cocoa beans as money to buy and sell goods at market. It was said that the beans were so precious that merchants picked up dropped beans as if they were their own eyes.

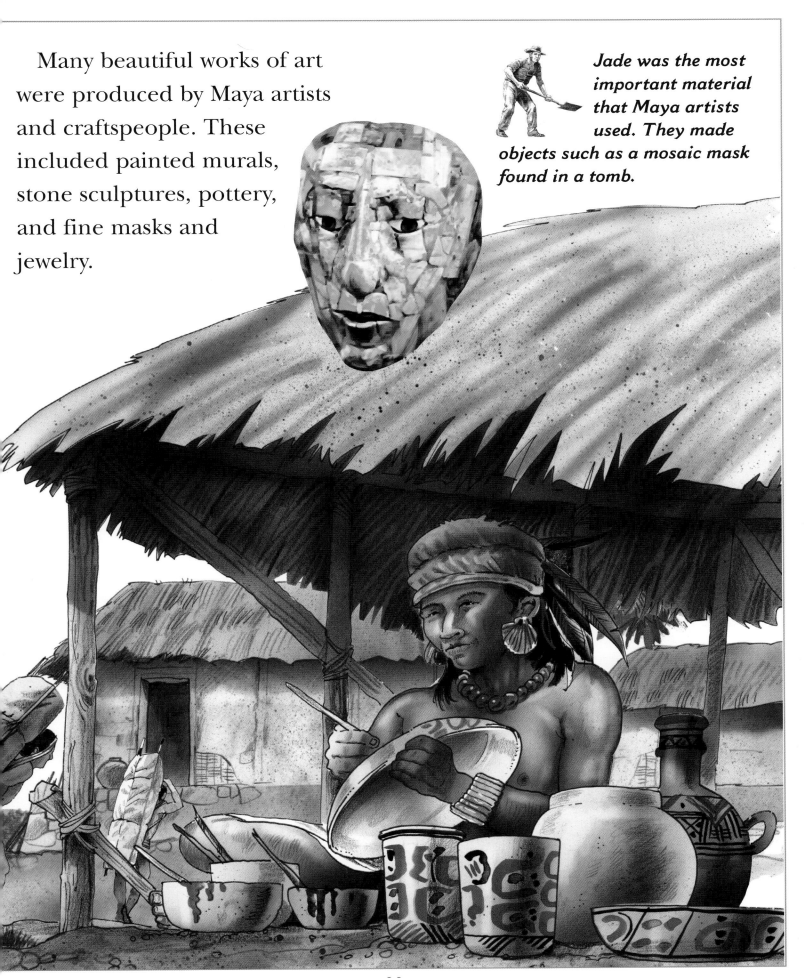

Many beautiful works of art were produced by Maya artists and craftspeople. These included painted murals, stone sculptures, pottery, and fine masks and jewelry.

Jade was the most important material that Maya artists used. They made objects such as a mosaic mask found in a tomb.

Family Life

Maya families usually lived together in one small house. Everyone in the household helped with the daily work.

Maya children did not go to school. Boys helped their fathers in the fields, and went with them on hunting and fishing trips.

Girls stayed at home with their mothers and learned how to cook, weave cloth, and look after the home.

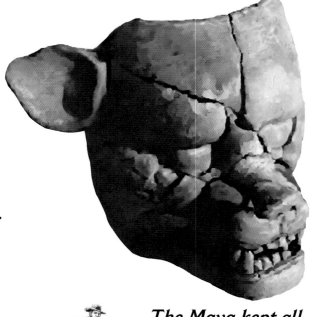

The Maya kept all kinds of dogs. Some were used for hunting. Others were fattened up and eaten, or sacrificed to the gods. Likenesses of dogs appear in pottery and other art.

Most Maya lived in small, simple houses built from wooden poles. The roofs were made with palm leaves or grass. A house had one main room, which had one area for cooking and eating, and another area for sleeping.

Women and girls wove cloth for the family's clothing from cotton and other plants. Cloth was woven on back looms that were fixed to a post with a strap around the weaver's back.

Maya children had toys such as a pottery whistle, shaped like a bird.

Clothes and Fashion

The clothes worn by the Maya were usually simple and well-suited to the warm weather.

Men wore loincloths. Women wore loose, long, smocklike dresses. Cloaks were worn if the weather got colder.

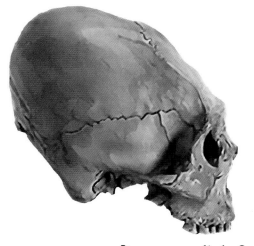

It was stylish for the Maya to be cross-eyed and have long heads. Babies had their heads strapped to make them change shape, and had beads dangled above their noses to alter their eye muscles.

Both rich (opposite page) and poor (left) Maya wore simple tunics and loincloths. But the poor did not have colorful clothes or jewelry.

Tattoos and body painting were very popular. Boys used black paint, and girls used red. Priests used blue for their tattoos, and warriors used red and black.

Rich Maya men and women liked to wear jewelry made from pieces of jade and seashells and headdresses made from colorful bird feathers.

The Maya sometimes filed their front teeth down into points and other patterns. They filled the gaps in their teeth with small pieces of jade.

What Happened to the Maya?

Between 1,000 and 800 years ago, Chichen Itza in Mexico became the most powerful city. Later, Mayapan took its place.

The Maya ruled until about 1,000 years ago, when people began to leave some of the cities and move into the highlands. Lots of things may have caused this. Lack of rain, overcrowding, war, and illness could all have been reasons.

Five hundred years later, in about 1520, the Spanish arrived in Central America. In less than 50 years, the Spanish had taken over almost all of the Maya lands.

Today the Maya no longer have cities, but they still live in the same parts of Central America and Mexico as their ancestors did.

The ruins of Maya cities have been found buried deep in the jungle. Many tourists visit them every year.

Maya people today keep some of their ancestors' customs alive. They still farm in the same way and grow maize on small plots of land. They also speak in ways based on the old Maya languages.

Glossary

astronomy—the study of planets, stars, and other objects in space

hieroglyphs—writing made up of pictures

jade—a semi-precious green stone

loincloths—clothing worn by Maya men, made from strips of cloth tied around their waists and passed between their legs

merchants—people who buy and sell things in order to make money

mosaic—a pattern made from tiny pieces of stone or tile

murals—wall paintings

peccary—a small wild pig found in Central America

sacred—important to someone's religion or beliefs

stelae—large stones used as a surface for writing

trade—buying and selling of goods such as jewelry and food

Further Resources

AT THE LIBRARY

Coulter, Laurie. *Secrets in Stone: All About Maya Hieroglyphs.* Boston, Mass.: Little, Brown, 2001.

Lourie, Peter. *The Mystery of the Maya: Uncovering the Lost City of Palenque.* Honesdale, Pa.: Boyds Mills Press, 2001.

Orr, Tamra. *The Maya.* New York: Franklin Watts, 2005.

ON THE WEB

For more information on the *Ancient Maya,* use FactHound

to track down Web sites related to this book.

   1. Go to *www.facthound.com*

   2. Type in a search word related to this book

      or this book ID: 0756516773

   3. Click on the *Fetch It* button.

FactHound will find the best Web sites for you.

LOOK FOR MORE BOOKS IN THIS SERIES

ANCIENT GREEKS
ISBN 0-7565-1646-3

ANCIENT ROMANS
ISBN 0-7565-1644-7

THE VIKINGS
ISBN 0-7565-1678-1

Index